CONTENTS

KT-116-169

Any words appearing in the text in bold, **like this,** are explained in the Glossary. You can also look out for them in the Up To Speed box at the bottom of each page.

WHAT ARE WARPLANES?

The air show crowd is getting restless. An F-15 Eagle fighter is due to make an appearance but it is nowhere to be seen. Then, a distant whine is heard. Eyes scan the sky. Within a second a jet comes crashing though the air to swoop low over the crowd with an ear-piercing roar.

The ground shakes as one of the most expensive machines on Earth thunders overhead. The plane loops, twists and turns. Then it stands on its tail and shoots to the top of the sky. In less than a minute it is gone. All that's left is the strong whiff of burned fuel. Seeing such an extraordinary sight, it is hard to believe that the first planes only flew a century ago.

THE FRENCH NIEUPORT 17

This was one of the first fighters of World War I. It could fly at 190 km/h (120 mph). It had a **machine gun** mounted on the top wing above the cockpit. The pilot could fire the gun while sitting but he had to stand up to reload with ammunition.

UP TO SPEED machine gun gun that can fire bullets in very rapid succession

FIGHTERS AND BOMBERS

During World War I (1914–18) two main types of warplane were invented. One type was the fighter – designed to destroy other enemy aircraft and gain control of the sky. The other type was the bomber – made to drop explosives on the enemy's troops, cities and factories.

Warplanes were also used for **reconnaissance** (spotting what the enemy are doing), ground support (helping troops fighting on the ground), and to transport supplies. Today, it is impossible to imagine fighting a war without aircraft but they have changed a lot since World War I.

A US air force F-15E Eagle in action, during the Gulf War of 1991.

FIND OUT LATER...

*Which plane can fly over three times the **speed of sound**?*

How do jet pilots learn to fly?

Which aircraft can somersault through the sky?

reconnaissance   keeping watch on an enemy's movements and strength

AERIAL BASICS

From the first clumsy **biplanes** to the latest jets, warplanes throughout the 20th century have had a lot in common. Fighters have to be fast and highly **manoeuvrable**. This gives the pilot the best possible chance to survive in a fight with an enemy. Bombers have to travel long distances and carry heavy loads. The labels marked on the RAF Tornado below show the names of important aircraft parts.

PROPELLER ENGINE

The first aircraft used engines similar to those in cars. These are called **internal combustion** engines. They work by exploding a small amount of fuel which moves a **piston**. This turns a **crankshaft** which then spins a **propeller**. The spinning propeller pulls the aircraft through the air.

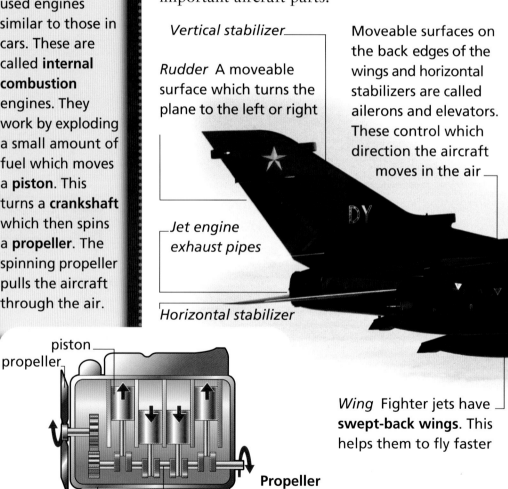

Vertical stabilizer

Rudder A moveable surface which turns the plane to the left or right

Moveable surfaces on the back edges of the wings and horizontal stabilizers are called ailerons and elevators. These control which direction the aircraft moves in the air

Jet engine exhaust pipes

Horizontal stabilizer

piston

propeller

Wing Fighter jets have **swept-back wings**. This helps them to fly faster

Propeller engine

crankcase

crankshaft

UP TO SPEED   manoeuvrable   able to turn or change direction easily

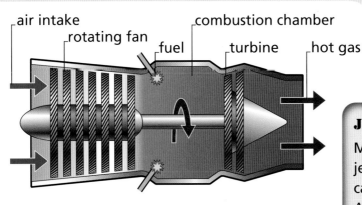

air intake
rotating fan
combustion chamber
fuel
turbine
hot gas

Turbojet engine

JET ENGINE
Modern military jets have engines called turbojets. Air is sucked into them through a fan, and then squeezed into a combustion chamber. Fuel mixes in with the air and **ignites**. Hot gases rush out of the back and drive the jet forward.

Ejector seat All jet fighter planes have special seats that can fire the crew away from the aircraft in an emergency

Fuselage The main body of the aircraft

The tip of a plane is called its nose. Some fighter jets have a powerful gun, or **cannon**, in the nose

Cockpit The crew sits in here

Insignia These markings show friend and enemy which country the plane is from

Weapons load Most modern jets carry missiles and bombs underneath their wings and fuselage

Air intake Air is sucked in here and into the jet engine

swept-back wings wings shaped like a paper dart

LEARNING TO FLY

Flying military aircraft has always been risky. In World War I half of all the 22,000 British pilots who flew in the war were killed. Many of them died in flying accidents. Flying warplanes can still be a highly dangerous job – with or without a war to fight. Ever since planes first took to the sky, learning how to fly them has been a matter of a trainer and learner going up together. Special trainer aircraft are used with dual controls. The first solo flight is one of the most nerve-racking experiences in a pilot's life.

FLIGHT PIONEERS

These American World War I pilots are learning to fly combat aircraft. Despite the terrible dangers, they were not issued with parachutes. The idea was to make them try and bring down even a badly damaged aircraft safely, rather than jump out of it.

Pilots learn to fly the Harrier VTOL jet with this two-seater version.

propeller   spinning blade that pulls an aircraft through the air

JET BOYS AND GIRLS

Learning to fly military jets is a long and difficult process. Trainee pilots have to be physically tough to put up with the stresses of being flung around the sky in a plane. They also need to have perfect eyesight and colour vision. Trainees start off on slow-moving **propeller** aircraft before moving to trainer jets. Finally they move up to two-seater versions of the powerful military aircraft they are going to fly. Even when a trainee is a proper pilot he or she still spends a lot of flying time on training exercises. These develop the skills picked up while learning to fly.

TOP OF THE RANGE VIDEO GAME

Today, pilots do part of their training on hi-tech computer-controlled flight simulators. A video screen projects a realistic image of what it is like looking out of a cockpit window. The flight simulator moves around like a real plane when the trainee moves the controls.

9

FLYING HERO

Douglas Bader, below, was a British fighter pilot who lost both his legs in a flying accident in 1931. He was not going to let that stop him fly. He became a Squadron Leader in the Battle of Britain in 1940. He was shot down in 1941 and captured by the Germans. He tried to escape from his **prison of war camp** several times but did not succeed.

ACES AND HEROES

World War I was like a nightmare for the soldiers of both sides. They lived and fought in muddy trenches. Millions of men were killed by **machine guns, artillery** shells and poison gas. Fighter pilots were different. They fought each other one to one in the clean blue sky. It was in this war that the idea of the 'ace' first came up. French pilots had to shoot down five enemy planes to be called an ace. German and British pilots had to shoot down ten.

▶▶▶▶▶▶▶▶▶▶▶
Find out more about the Battle of Britain on page 15.

THE RED BARON

The most famous ace of World War I was the German, Manfred von Richthofen. He was known as the Red Baron, after the colour of the red Fokker Dreidecker **triplane** he flew. During the war, the Red Baron shot down 80 planes belonging to the **Allies**. He flew with a **squadron** known as Richthofen's Flying Circus, because the planes were brightly coloured. He was shot down and killed behind British lines at the end of the war.

World War II had its share of aces, too. The most successful was the German pilot Erich Hartmann. He shot down 352 Russian planes.

GLAMOROUS GLENNIS

Chuck Yeager was an American **test pilot**. In 1947 he became the first person to fly an aircraft faster than the **speed of sound**. He made the flight in the **rocket-propelled** X-1. This was called *Glamorous Glennis*, after his wife. At the time, flying at such speeds was very dangerous. Planes would fall apart in flight, or go into uncontrollable spins that ended in fiery explosions.

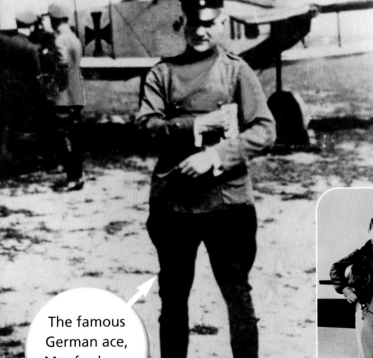

The famous German ace, Manfred von Richthofen.

triplane   plane with three sets of wings on each side

FIGHTERS

Military men quickly got the idea that planes could help them fight wars. They were first used in World War I as **reconnaissance** aircraft. Soldiers heading for positions on the **front line** soon came to dread the noise of an enemy aircraft above their heads. After the aircraft had gone, they could expect attack. Reconnaissance planes were such a problem that a new kind of aircraft was invented to drive them from the sky – the fighter.

FOUR WINGS

Most warplanes of World War I were **biplanes**. This means they had two sets of wings. This Sopwith Camel was a successful British design. Aircraft like this were used to defend London from German Gotha bombers.

biplane   plane with two sets of wings, one above the other

WORLD WAR I FIGHTERS

In World War I pilots first fought each other with pistols, rifles or even grappling hooks (hooks rather like an anchor on the end of a rope or chain). Not surprisingly, these weapons did not cause a lot of damage.

Machine guns, firing hundreds of bullets a minute, were far better weapons. These were fitted on the top wing, or in a second cockpit behind the pilot. Just in front of the pilot should have been the best place to put the guns. He could then point his plane at the enemy and fire. But, at the start of the war, this would have meant shooting his own propeller off.

Fokker Dr.1 **triplanes** – one of the most **manoeuvrable** fighters of their time.

FIRING THROUGH THE PROPELLER

The then-German (now Dutch) Fokker aircraft company solved the problem of firing through the **propeller** in 1915. They invented a device that timed the firing of bullets so they passed between the propeller blades. The picture above shows an early US version of this type of machine gun.

---

front line   place on a battlefield where the two sides meet
manoeuvrable   able to turn or change direction easily

WORLD WAR II FIGHTERS

Fighter planes changed a lot in the 20 years between the two World Wars. Open cockpits were covered with a **perspex** screen. This meant pilots had a less chilly and wind-battered flight. Instead of two sets of wings, most planes had one set. The fighter's guns were usually inside the wing. The pilot fired them by a control in the cockpit, rather than by pulling the trigger himself. These fighters were also considerably faster and deadlier than the planes of World War I.

LITTLE FRIENDS

The P-51 Mustang, made by a company called North American, was one of the best US fighter planes of the war. Its job was to protect slow-moving bombers from German and Japanese fighters. It carried extra fuel in tear-shaped pods under the wings. This allowed it to fly for up to eight hours. By the end of the war, Mustangs could fly with US bombers from England to Berlin in Germany.

This picture shows a Spitfire (front) during the Battle of Britain.

perspex   transparent, tough, plastic-like resin, used instead of glass to make windows or cockpit covers in aircraft

BATTLE OF BRITAIN

The first full-scale air battle in history was fought in the summer of 1940. It was called the Battle of Britain. The German air force tried to destroy the British air force. If they had succeeded, Germany would have gone on to invade and conquer Britain. Fortunately, the British air force had two excellent fighter planes called the Hurricane and the Spitfire. The Hurricane was steady, rugged and effective. The Spitfire was so fast and **manoeuvrable** it could fly rings around its opponents. Many people think it is one of the most beautiful aircraft ever built.

FAST BUT FATAL

The Japanese Mitsubishi A6M Zero was one of the fastest and most manoeuvrable fighters of the Pacific war. But there was a catch. To save weight to help it fly faster, it had no armour to protect the pilot. It carried no radio, and had a fuel tank that often burst into flames. Japanese fighter pilots discovered that their zippy Zero could be shot down very easily.

MODERN JET FIGHTERS

The first military jets were flown by the Germans near the end of the World War II. The German air force attacked US bomber formations with the Me 262. This two-engine jet was almost impossible to shoot down because it moved so much faster than any other plane in the sky. Surprisingly, pilots of the Me 262 found it difficult to shoot down the slow-moving bombers. They did not have enough time to line up their planes to get an accurate shot as they zoomed past. The first battles between jets took place during the Korean War (1950–53).

TOP SELLER

The MiG-21 is the best-selling jet fighter ever made. During the **Cold War** the Russians built more than 15,000. They sold the planes to countries all over the world.

Cold War   years between 1946 and 1989 when Soviet Russia and the USA and its allies did not like or trust each other

SPEED OF SOUND

Jet engines became more powerful after World War II. It was soon possible for aircraft to fly faster than the **speed of sound**. It is now common for jet fighters to fly at 1600 **km/h** (1000 **mph**) or more. Single-seater jet fighters, such as the American F-16 or Russian MiG-25, now weigh as much as a World War II bomber did. They are much more complicated pieces of machinery. These amazing planes can travel 1000 metres in less than 2 seconds.

The F-16 – one of the most effective fighters ever.

SP
AF 9 415

VTOL JETS

Aircraft need a runway to land and take off. This can be awkward for military aircraft. A runway near the enemy's **front line** is large and **vulnerable** to air attack and **artillery**. Helicopters can take off and land from a much smaller area, but they are no match for any **high-performance**, enemy jet fighter. This is why the **vertical** take-off and landing (VTOL) jet is such a useful idea. These aircraft can take off and land straight upwards and downwards like helicopters.

A DREAM TO FLY?

This weird and wonderful machine was an early British experiment in vertical take-off aircraft. It was nicknamed the 'Flying Bedstead'.

artillery   large, land-based guns

HOVER CRAFT

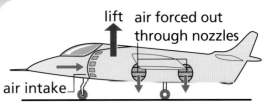

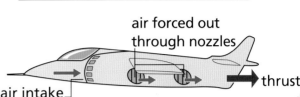

Like a helicopter, a VTOL jet can take off and land in a very tight space. Also similar to a helicopter, it can hover in the air. These aircraft first appeared in the 1960s when the British and Russian air forces each had their own version. The Russians had the Yakovlev Yak 36. The British had the Hawker Siddeley Harrier jump jet. The American military also bought the Harrier. The Harrier cannot fly as fast as most other modern jet fighters but it is very **manoeuvrable** and is a good combat aircraft.

HOW THE ENGINE WORKS

The Harrier jet **thrust** comes out of four rotating **nozzles** on the side of the aircraft. When the pilot wants to take off or land, he places the nozzles in a downward position. When the pilot wants to fly forward, the nozzles point backward.

A Harrier VTOL jet takes off from a US **aircraft carrier**.

thrust force produced by a jet aircraft to propel it through the sky
vulnerable easy to attack or shoot down, not well protected

19

BOMBERS

The first **strategic bombers** were strange, gas-filled balloons, the size of cruise ships. They were called Zeppelins, after their inventor and manufacturer Count Ferdinand von Zeppelin. Instead of wings, they used massive bags of hydrogen to lift them into the air. They also had **propeller** engines to push them through the sky. They could travel for hundreds of miles without refuelling. At first the Germans built them as **reconnaissance** craft for the navy. Then they decided to use them to drop bombs on enemy cities.

IN CONTROL

The control cabin of a Zeppelin (see below) was cold and very noisy. When the Zeppelin's engines were running, the crew could barely hear themselves speak. There were no seats or parachutes. This saved weight for important cargo such as bombs.

A Zeppelin on the way to attack England.

ATTACK AND DEFENCE

The first Zeppelin raids took place on Paris and London in 1915. They caused a lot of fear and panic among the helpless people below but much less damage than intended. This was because Zeppelins could carry only a small number of bombs. At first these awe-inspiring machines were impossible to shoot down. They flew too high for fighters to reach. But by late 1916 British fighters such as the BE-2 **biplane** could catch up with them. Pilots fighting Zeppelins fired **incendiary bullets** from **machine guns**. These bullets glowed white hot when shot from the gun. They set fire to the hydrogen gas inside the Zeppelin. This caused a huge explosion that destroyed it.

THE CLOUD CAR
This tiny carriage contained a member of the crew. It dangled from a Zeppelin hidden in a cloud, out of sight of enemy aircraft or anti-aircraft guns. The man inside the cloud car used a telephone line to the Zeppelin's pilot to guide the craft along.

strategic bomber bomber that attacks an enemy's home territory, rather than being used on the battlefield

21

WORLD WAR I BOMBERS

Zeppelins terrified the people of enemy cities. But they were slow and very expensive. They became easy to shoot down and could only carry a small number of bombs. So the countries fighting World War I began to invent aircraft that could travel faster, carry more bombs and be more difficult to shoot down. The first winged bombers were magnificent but clumsy-looking machines, such as the German Zeppelin-Staaken R, and the British Handley Page 0/100. These aircraft could carry a deadly load of up to 1800 kg of bombs. They also had room for three or more machine gunners to defend the bomber from attacking fighters.

DON'T HIT THE WING!

The first bombers were ordinary **reconnaissance** or fighter planes. The pilot or air gunner lobbed a couple of hand-held bombs out of his open cockpit. These missiles were hardly more destructive than a hand grenade.

Gotha bombers such as this, attacked Paris and London.

   reconnaissance   keeping watch on an enemy's movements and strength

DROPPING BOMBS

During World War I, the bomber's pilot or air gunner dropped the first bombs from the aircraft's open cockpit. Later, bombs were fitted under the wings.

By 1918, specially built bombers had their own bomb bay. This was a section of the plane designed to carry bombs. Aircraft like these had a crew of four or more men. Not all World War I bombers were like these sturdy planes. Some, like the British Sopwith 1½ Strutter or French Breguet 14, were almost the same size as fighters. They had only one or two pilots, and carried fewer bombs. Aircraft like these were much more **manoeuvrable,** so they were harder to shoot down.

CREATURES OF THE NIGHT

The big World War I bombers, such as this Handley Page 0/400, were slow and clumsy. This made them easy targets for enemy fighters or anti-aircraft fire. Because of this, bombers usually operated at night, when it was far more difficult to spot them.

WORLD WAR II BOMBERS

Bombers had almost no effect on the countries that fought World War I. But in World War II they destroyed whole cities.

World War II bombers still had propeller engines but other than that they changed almost completely. Their crews flew inside the planes, rather than in seats open to the air. Instead of a **machine gun** mounted on a rack in an open cockpit, two or four machines guns were inside **perspex turrets**. They carried a lot more bombs. The British Handley Page 0/400 bomber of World War I carried 816 kg of bombs. The Avro Lancaster, its World War II equivalent, carried at least 6350 kg.

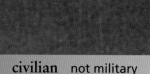

TOO SLOW FOR COMFORT

The German Heinkel He 111 was used successfully at the start of the war, in Poland and Western Europe. But during the Battle of Britain in 1940, the He 111 and other German bombers were too slow and clumsy for faster British fighters (such as the Supermarine Spitfire and the Hawker Hurricane).

civilian   not military

LONG-RANGE BOMBERS

The most effective bombers of the war were large four-engine aircraft such as the American Boeing B-17 Flying Fortress and Consolidated B-24 Liberator, and the British Handley Page Halifax and Avro Lancaster. They made medium to long-range journeys. Sometimes hundreds of these aircraft took off from Britain's east coast to fly over Germany. Raids like these destroyed cities such as Dresden and Hamburg, and killed hundreds of thousands of **civilians**.

At the end of the war, the US air force began using long-range bombers called Boeing B-29 Superfortresses. The B-29 could fly half-way across the Pacific Ocean (three times as far as a B-17). It dropped **incendiary bombs** to destroy Japan's cities, which were built mainly of wood.

A Boeing B-17 Flying Fortress over enemy territory in 1944.

incendiary bomb   bomb that bursts into flames, rather than explodes

THE FIRST ATOMIC BOMBER

An American B-29 called the *Enola Gay* dropped the first atomic bomb. Here the pilot is standing next to the plane before the mission. After the bomb attack, one of the crew described the city below as looking like a pot of boiling black oil.

NUCLEAR BOMBERS

World War II began in 1939 with **squadrons** of German bombers destroying large areas of the Polish capital of Warsaw. It ended in 1945 with two single bombers dropping a bomb each on the Japanese cities of Hiroshima and Nagasaki. Both cities were completely destroyed. The bombs were atomic bombs. It had cost two billion dollars for scientists in the USA to make them. In 1949 the Soviet Union (Russia and the states it controlled) tested its own atomic bomb. In the early 1950s both the USA and Russia developed the hydrogen bomb. This was a new type of atomic weapon. Such bombs were 750 times more powerful than the ones that destroyed Hiroshima and Nagasaki.

interceptor   type of jet fighter that can climb and fly very quickly to cut off (intercept) enemy aircraft

A Soviet Tu-95 'Bear' (top) nuclear bomber shadowed by US planes.

MID-AIR DRINK

Nuclear bombers make such long journeys that they often need to take on extra fuel while they are flying. The British invented this technique. This picture shows a B-47 bomber taking fuel from a tanker aircraft.

AVOIDING ENEMY FIRE

After World War II the USA and Russia became enemies. They did not fight, but a deep dislike grew up between them. This was known as the **Cold War**. Both sides had plans to attack each other with hydrogen bombs. Long-range bombers were invented to fly across **continents** carrying these weapons. These bombers had to fly high and fast. They needed to avoid enemy **interceptor** fighters, and anti-aircraft guns and missiles from the ground. By the 1960s, **intercontinental ballistic missiles** (**ICBMs**) were invented to carry hydrogen bombs from one continent to another without pilots. They could be fired from underground **silos** or **submarines**, and nuclear bombers became less important.

squadron   fighting group or unit in an air force

RUSSIAN SWING-WING

The Tu-22M/Tu-26 'Backfire' is the Russian swing-wing equivalent to the American F-111. This aircraft can take 12,000 kg of bombs 12,000 kilometres (7500 miles).

SWING-WING JETS

Many jet fighters and bombers have **swept-back wings**. This makes a V or triangular shape against the body of the plane. The jets have this design because this wing shape helps the aircraft fly faster. But swept-back wings have one big problem. They do not offer as much **lift** as wings that stick out more. This is especially difficult when the aircraft is taking off or landing. Such jets need long runways and have to travel a long way at high speed before they can take off.

An F-111 swing-wing bomber with its wings swept forward.

TECH TALK

Wings

All plane wings have a special curved shape. Air rushes under the bottom of the wing at a higher pressure than air rushing over the top. This produces lift, which gets a plane off the ground.

WINGS OUT

The problem was solved in the early 1960s with the invention of **swing-wing** jets. For take-off and landing, these jets bring their wings forward (and out). This means they can take off and land in shorter distances and at lower, safer speeds than if they had their wings swept-back. This is especially useful for planes flying long distances, as a plane always uses a large amount of fuel to get itself into the air.

WINGS IN

Early swing-wing jets such as the American F-111 and Russian Tupolev Tu-22M/Tu-26 'Backfire' needed to fly high and fast, with wings back (or in), until they had almost reached their target areas. Then they would sneak down very low and slow, with wings forward, under an enemy's **radar**, to launch missiles or drop bombs.

> > > > > > > > > > > >
Find out more about radar on page 53.

SWING-WINGS IN ACTION

OUT
The jet can take off or land at a safe speed.

IN
The jet flies high and fast, escaping enemy attack and getting where it wants to go quickly.

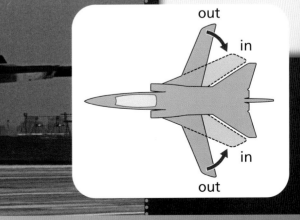

radar   way of finding out position of objects, like aircraft, using radio signals

SMALL BOMBERS

Modern bombers carry many different weapons. These modern weapons can hit their targets accurately. This means they keep damage of non-military buildings to a minimum, and cut down on **civilian** casualties.

There are two main types of modern jet bomber. One is the smaller medium-range aircraft such as the Anglo-French (built by Britain and France together) Jaguar or Tornado. Aircraft like these are 'multi-role'. As well as working as bombers, they are fast and agile enough to be fighters, **reconnaissance** aircraft, and ground-support (giving back-up to troops on the ground) aircraft. They are not much bigger than a jet fighter. Still, they can carry a weapons load as large as a World War II bomber such as the B-17 Flying Fortress.

WHERE'S THE TAIL?

The tailless Northrop Grumman B-2A Spirit stealth bomber is the latest stealth design. It is much bigger than the Nighthawks flying with it. It is said to be almost impossible to shoot down, but at over 2 **billion** US dollars a plane, it should be quite special.

BIG BOMBERS

The most famous large bomber is the American Boeing B-52 Stratofortress, which has a range of over 14,080 kilometres (8800 miles). This bomber first flew in 1952, and it is expected to still be in use in 2040!

The most modern bombers have features that make them hard to spot by enemy **radar**. The shape of the F-117 Nighthawk **stealth** fighter makes it look much smaller on a radar screen than it really is. Its special paint is also designed to soak up radar waves so it does not reflect back a strong signal.

THE EUROPEAN TORNADO

Introduced in the early 1980s, this small two-crew aircraft can fly in all weather and reach targets 1300 km (800 mi.) away. Small bombers like this can do much more than big bombers such as the B-52. The B-52 can carry 4500 kg (5 tons) of bombs. The Tornado can carry 8000 kg (9 tons) of mixed bombs and missiles.

A US air force F-117 Nighthawk stealth fighter.

stealth   designed to not be seen

ALL AT SEA

GIANT KILLER

Before World War II, the thought of single-engine aircraft destroying a battleship seemed ridiculous. But during the attack on Pearl Harbor, fleets of Nakajima B5N 'Kate' attack bombers did just that. Most of the ships were sunk by torpedoes from 'Kates'.

The first take-off from a ship happened in 1910 on the American cruiser USS *Birmingham*. Warplanes were soon being used for **reconnaissance**. They also attacked some enemy ships or other targets.

AIRCRAFT CARRIERS

The first **aircraft carriers** were built during World War I, but too late to play a major part in the war. Between World Wars I and II, the USA, Japan and Britain built up aircraft carrier forces. Japan used hers to open World War II in the Pacific. The result was devastating.

This replica 'Kate' was used in the film *Tora! Tora! Tora!*

aircraft carrier   warship that carries fighter planes to near their target, like a mobile airfield

PEARL HARBOR

On 7 December 1941, 183 Japanese planes from six aircraft carriers attacked the American navy and air base of Pearl Harbor, Hawaii. The time was just before 8.00 a.m. An hour later, another force of 167 planes from the same carriers arrived for another attack. The aircraft carried bombs and **torpedoes**. Between them, they sank or seriously damaged eighteen US warships. They also destroyed 174 US aircraft. The attack was one of the most important air battles in history. While the USA was recovering, Japanese soldiers invaded and took over huge amounts of territory in the Pacific ocean.

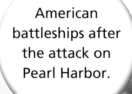

American battleships after the attack on Pearl Harbor.

UNWILLING HERO

Japanese admiral Yamamoto Isoroku planned the Pearl Harbor attack. It was a great success. But he was never convinced that going to war against the USA was a good idea. When he was congratulated on the success of the attack, he said, 'I fear we have only awakened a sleeping tiger.' He meant that Japan would now have to fight the huge power of the USA, which it had not had to do before.

torpedo   long, thin, underwater bomb that uses a propeller to push it along

33

CARRIER FORCES

Aircraft carriers are a wonder of the modern age. After Pearl Harbor, the USA's carrier forces helped win the war against Japan in the Pacific. Today, the USA has the greatest carrier force in the world. These carriers have been used very effectively in both Gulf Wars. They launch jet aircraft on bombing missions into enemy territory. They have their own supply of **cruise missiles**. Russia, Britain, France and other nations also have carrier forces. They use them to back up their military forces in trouble spots around the world.

Aircraft carriers can travel to almost anywhere on the planet to help out a nation's troops.

The US aircraft carrier *John F. Kennedy* passes through the Caribbean.

SWORDFISH

Biplanes still operated during World War II. This British Fairey Swordfish was a carrier-based **torpedo** bomber. In 1941 a **squadron** of Swordfish helped to destroy the German battleship, *Bismarck*. This was the biggest ship in the German navy at the time. Sinking her was very important to the British.

　biplane　plane with two sets of wings, one above the other

TOP SHIPS

A large, modern aircraft carrier is over 330 metres (1000 feet) long. It can carry 90 or so aircraft. It takes over 3000 men to look after the ship, and another 3000 to look after the aircraft. Because aircraft carriers are so important, they usually travel with a fleet of other ships. Cruisers and destroyers (smaller, highly mobile and well-armed ships) protect them from enemy ships, aircraft and ground-launched missiles. Supply ships keep them equipped with fuel, ammunition and food.

PHANTOM STRIKE

The McDonnell Douglas F-4 Phantom was one of the USA's most useful carrier-based fighter-bombers, during the 1960s and 70s. It carried several different missiles. Some missiles were meant for ground targets, and others were to protect it from enemy aircraft.

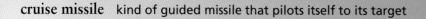

cruise missile   kind of guided missile that pilots itself to its target

FLYING-BOATS

Flying-boats may look clumsy, but because they land on water they have two great advantages over land-based planes. First, their pilots never have to worry about running out of runway for landing and take-off.

Second, flying-boats can land facing in any direction. It is difficult to land an ordinary plane on a runway if there is a strong wind blowing across it. The first military flying-boats were built during World War I. In the 1930s aircraft designers made planes that were much bigger than those that could fly from land.

AMPHIBIOUS WONDER

More American Catalina flying-boats were made than any other kind of flying-boat. The Catalina could operate from both land and sea, because it had an undercarriage (**landing gear**) as well as a boat-like hull and floats on its wings.

　　landing gear　wheels and lower part of an aircraft that support it when it takes off or lands

FLYING PORCUPINES

Britain, Japan and the USA all had flying-boat fleets during World War II. They were used for **reconnaissance**, rescue missions for airmen stranded in the sea, and for attacking enemy ships and **submarines**. The vast Short Sunderland flying-boat shown here had a crew of thirteen. It dropped bombs or **depth charges** on enemy submarines. It was extremely good at fighting off enemy planes. German airmen called it 'the flying porcupine'. It was a slow flyer (341 **km/h**/212 **mph**), but it could stay in the air for 20 hours. Unlike some flying boats, the Sunderland could only land and take off from water. It only left the water to be repaired.

A lumbering Sunderland flying-boat being repaired during World War II.

UNDERWATER PLANES

During World War II, Japan and the USA used submarines as **aircraft carriers**. The Japanese submarines carried three **torpedo** bombers. The submarine was designed to launch surprise attacks on America's west coast, but it was never used to do this.

submarine ship that can stay underwater

EYES IN THE SKY

BALLOONS

Since warfare began, army commanders have wanted to be able to see what their enemy was doing. By 600AD the Chinese had invented huge kites to lift a man into the air to see much further than anyone on the ground. In 1783, a Frenchman named Jacques Charles invented the hydrogen balloon. Almost at once French army commanders took up the idea. Hydrogen balloons were used to spy on enemy armies during the Napoleonic Wars. These balloons could be blown anywhere by the wind, so were tied down to keep them in one place. Balloons like these were used throughout the nineteenth century, and during World War I.

SPOTTER PLANES

The **reconnaissance** balloon's days were numbered once powered flight was invented. Balloons were already **vulnerable** to powerful, long-range **artillery**. They were easy targets for fighter planes. One of the first reconnaissance planes was the British BE 2, used in World War I. It was a slow and steady flyer, which made it just right for spotting enemy movements from the sky. This also made it very easy to shoot down. Some of the reconnaissance planes used in World War II were specially built for the job. The weird and wonderful World War II Blohm & Voss Bv 141 had an all-round-visibility glass cabin. It was one of the strangest aircraft ever made.

WOODEN PLANE

This British De Havilland Mosquito was one of the most successful reconnaissance aircraft of World War II. Because it was made of wood it was very light, and could outrun any German fighter until the arrival of the Messerschmidt Me 262 jet in late 1944.

The strange shape of the Blohm & Voss Bv 141 reconnaissance plane.

reconnaissance   keeping watch on an enemy's movements and strength
vulnerable   easy to attack or shoot down, not well protected

39

SEEING SOUND

The shockwave created as an aircraft breaks the sound barrier is sometimes seen for a split-second as a cloud of condensation. This amazing picture of an F/A-18 Hornet shows that moment, which is heard as a boom.

COLD WAR SPIES

In the **Cold War** between Russia and the USA and its **allies** after World War II, special aircraft were developed by both sides to spy on the enemy. One of the most famous was the American U2. It could not fly fast, and pilots hoped that flying at high **altitude** (24,400 metres/ 80,000 feet) would keep it safe from attack. This did not always work and some U2s were shot down by missiles. Another US **reconnaissance** plane was the Lockheed SR-71 Blackbird. Some people think it is the most beautiful jet ever made. The Blackbird had a top speed of Mach 3, and was crammed with **radar** and photography equipment. It was too fast for fighters and missiles to shoot down.

altitude   height above sea level
obsolete   old-fashioned, out-of-date

A Lockheed SR-71 Blackbird shoots through the sky.

SUBMARINE SPOTTERS

Both sides in the Cold War built special reconnaissance planes to hunt **submarines**. The British-built Nimrod was one of these aircraft. The Nimrod could fly 12-hour missions without refuelling. It had several detection devices to spot submarines, including one that was dragged through the sea under the aircraft. The Nimrod was equipped with anti-submarine mines, bombs and **torpedoes**. Today, satellites and pilotless planes provide a lot of useful military information on other countries. The manned reconnaissance plane may soon be **obsolete**.

MOBILE RADAR

This jet carries a huge radar bowl on its back. Such aircraft are known as AWACS planes. This stands for Airborne Warning and Control System. During the Cold War they kept a lookout for unexpected missile attacks.

torpedo   a long, thin, underwater bomb that uses a propeller to push it along

41

ATTACK AND SUPPORT

Soldiers have had to put up with attack from the air since the days of World War I. Slow **biplane** fighters would fire **machine guns** from above. This was called 'strafing', which comes from a German word meaning 'punish'. But although it was effective, strafing enemy trenches (the deep ditches dug to protect soldiers) was a highly dangerous job. Many planes were shot down, or their pilots badly injured by ground fire.

STUKA SIREN

This German dive bomber from World War II had special sirens fitted to its wings. When it dived down to drop its single bomb, the sirens gave a piercing wail that was meant to spread panic among the soldiers below.

GROUND ATTACK

In World War II ground attack aircraft included the German Stuka and Russian Shturmovik. They caused panic among the troops and tank crews they were sent to attack.

UP TO SPEED cannon   weapon similar to a machine gun, but using larger bullets

THUNDERBOLT

Today, ground attack aircraft are still a vital part of warfare. The A-10 Thunderbolt is one of the most well known. It was used in both Gulf Wars. It is a slow, clumsy-looking airplane, but it is built to withstand enemy fire. The pilot is surrounded by heavy armour. It is highly **manoeuvrable,** and can make very tight turns. The Thunderbolt carries an amazing number of weapons – over 7000 kilograms ($7\frac{1}{2}$ tons) including cluster bombs and anti-tank missiles. It is also armed with a **cannon** that can fire 4200 rounds per minute. That is 70 heavy cannon shells a second – enough to give any tank commander nightmares.

The A-10 Thunderbolt may look bulky, but it can make sharp turns.

machine gun gun that can fire bullets in very rapid succession

PARACHUTES

The parachute was invented in the late eighteenth century. Parachute troops (paratroops) were first used in combat during World War II. Soldiers could be dropped behind enemy lines but a soldier floating slowly to earth was very **vulnerable**. Because of this, paratroops were usually dropped as low as possible to cut down on their time in the air.

The German army used paratroops to win a quick victory in Crete in 1941. British and US paratroops were dropped during the **D-Day** landings of 1944. Today, soldiers on the ground carry surface-to-air missiles that can easily bring down slow-moving aircraft. This means a massive parachute drop is unlikely because it is far too dangerous.

A Soviet TB 3 used to drop parachute troops.

commandos   small fighting force specially trained to make quick attacks into enemy areas

GLIDERS

Gliders, towed by heavy bombers, were used by both sides in World War II. They carried supplies and troops. A large glider could even carry a tank. But gliders were very slow, and crashed easily on landing.

One of the most famous uses of gliders was in 1943. Germany's Italian **ally** Mussolini was held captive by his own government. Hitler sent German **commandos** to rescue him. Gliders landed silently by the mountaintop hotel where Mussolini was being held. Then troops stormed into the building. The attack was such a surprise that not a single shot was fired. Mussolini was flown away in a small German **reconnaissance** plane.

D-DAY GLIDER

This Airspeed Horsa glider was used to carry Allied troops during the June 1944 D-Day landings. A bad landing could mean all aboard were killed.

D-Day 6th June 1944, day that the Allied invasion of mainland Europe began along the north coast of France

HELICOPTERS

The ground attack aircraft has a serious rival – the helicopter. The first helicopters were invented in the mid-1930s. They cannot fly as fast as airplanes, but they can take off and land in a small space. They can also hover (stay in one place) in the air, and are very **manoeuvrable**. During World War II, the US navy began to use helicopters for rescue missions at sea. Military helicopters are still used this way today. They also quickly ferry wounded soldiers back from the battlefield for medical attention behind the lines.

MEDEVACS

Around 7000 of these Bell Huey helicopters flew in Vietnam, for 'dust offs' (dropping troops in enemy territory) and 'medevacs' (evacuating soldiers in need of medical aid).

The insect-like AH-64 Apache helicopter.

radar   way of finding out position of solid objects, like aircraft, by using radio signals

EASY TARGETS

Helicopters were first used in great numbers in the Vietnam War. Bell Hueys and Boeing Vertol Chinooks carried around supplies and took

troops into battle. These helicopters were able to take soldiers across countryside that ordinary vehicles could not get through. But helicopters had a downside too. They were easy to shoot down – even by rifle or **machine-gun** fire.

Today helicopters are also used as attack craft. The Boeing AH-64 Apache attack helicopter pictured here has **radar-**controlled missiles and guns for ground targets. It also has air-to-air missiles to protect it from other aircraft.

AIR FERRY

Boeing Vertol CH-47C Chinook transport helicopters also flew in Vietnam. They were important, too, in the Falklands War and both Gulf Wars. They ferried troops and equipment to places that were hard to get to any other way.

TRANSPORT

Some of the biggest aircraft ever built have been designed to carry troops and equipment across **continents** to distant battlefields. The first transporters were modified passenger planes, such as the German Ju52, or American DC-3 Dakota. Both were used with great success during World War II. Even larger transporters were designed during the **Cold War**. Military forces still use these today.

AIR MOBIL

civilian not military

Some transporters are just massive fuel tankers, such as this Boeing KC-135 Stratotanker. It first flew in the 1950s and has been used by the US air force ever since. It carries 55 tonnes of fuel.

BIG MOUTH

One of the largest transporters is the Lockheed C-5 Galaxy. This huge, jet-powered aircraft can carry 415 troops or 124,000 kilograms (137 tons) of equipment on its twin decks. It has 28 wheels to spread its massive weight over the ground. This makes it easier to land and take off from rough airstrips near a **front line**. Even fully loaded, it can fly nearly 5500 kilometres (3500 miles) in a single journey.

The US C-5 Galaxy transporter can carry a massive load.

Waiting fighters or bombers refuel in midair using a long pipe at the back of the aircraft. These tankers are very **vulnerable** so they operate at 15,000 m (50,000 ft). This keeps them out of reach of most fighters and enemy missiles.

◀ ◀ ◀ ◀ ◀ ◀ ◀ ◀ ◀ ◀
Find out more about the Ju52 on page 44.

front line   place on a battlefield where the two sides meet

TECHNOLOGY

In less than a hundred years, air weapons have changed almost completely. The first warplanes carried small hand-held bombs that could do very little damage.

ADVANCES IN TECHNOLOGY

By 1945 one bomber could destroy a city with a single atomic bomb. Today a single bomber packed with nuclear weapons could destroy an entire country and millions of its citizens. The first bombs were steel cylinders packed with explosives. They blew up when they hit the ground. Nothing guided them down once they had been dropped and they often missed their target.

BOUNCING BOMB

This famous bomb (shown being dropped below) from World War II was designed by British scientist Barnes Wallace. Its target was the great concrete dams in Germany's industrial centre. The bomb bounced like a ball across the water over nets placed in front of the dams.

A modern jet surrounded by its weapons **payload**.

radar   way of finding out position of objects, like aircraft, by using radio waves

GUIDED MISSILES

Today's military aircraft have guided missiles and smart bombs to attack targets on the ground. Weapons like this are directed to their targets by electronic guidance systems. These can be on-board TV cameras, or heat and **radar** tracking devices.

The Hellfire is a US missile that can be dropped by an aircraft. Soldiers on the ground or helicopters circling nearby guide it to its target. The idea is to make the most of an expensive weapon and cut down on **civilian** casualties. But smart bombs do not always work. If they miss, many civilians can be killed.

MOAB

During the war in Afghanistan in 2002, US forces dropped the biggest non-nuclear bomb available – the MOAB, or Massive Ordnance Air Burst. These 10-tonne (11-ton) cylinders, like the one below, carry a huge load that explodes above ground. They release a force big enough to knock over tanks and kill any soldier within several hundred metres.

WATCH OUT ABOVE

Ever since aircraft were first used in combat, their targets on the ground have been trying to fire back at them. Ground-to-air guns are usually called anti-aircraft guns. They were first used to shoot down enemy **reconnaissance** balloons. When the balloons went higher to escape the bullets, the men in them could not see what was happening on the ground. During World War I, anti-aircraft guns were used against aircraft and Zeppelins. They did not shoot many down, though. Hitting a fast-moving target, high up in the sky, was not easy.

A Sea Sparrow surface-to-air missile (SAM) launched from a carrier.

GETTING CLOSER

During World War II, German scientists developed a new kind of explosive weapon called the surface-to-air missile (SAM). It was a bomb that could move under its own power, rather than just dropping through the air. The first SAMs were either point-and-fire weapons with no **guidance**, or were radio-controlled. By the 1950s, SAMs had been invented that followed the heat given out by an aircraft's engines. Today, anti-aircraft SAMs pick up on **radar** signals from an enemy aircraft, or have small TV cameras in their noses, that allow people to guide them into their target. Some SAMs are so small they can be carried by a soldier.

TECH TALK

Radar
Radar equipment sends a strong radio signal into the sky. If the signal hits a plane, it bounces back to the radar. This signal shows up its position on a TV screen.

MULTI-BARREL MAYHEM

Bullets are still used to shoot at enemy aircraft. This Russian ZSU 30-4 tracks its target via radar and shoots all four barrels at once in a continuous stream of deadly fire.

An RAF Harrier pilot ejects just before the plane crashes.

BURNT OUT

The picture shows German troops inspecting the burning wreck of an American bomber shot down over Tunisia in 1943. When a bomber went down like this, it was rare that the whole crew would have time to escape.

BALE OUT!

In the early days of air warfare, pilots did not carry parachutes. This was to stop pilots baling out rather than trying to land their expensive flying machines in one piece. Zeppelin crews did not carry parachutes either. Although they were very big, Zeppelins could only lift a small load. The people in charge thought it was more important to carry bombs than parachutes.

By World War II, there was much more concern about keeping pilots safe. Parachutes were given to pilots in almost all air forces. If a plane was badly damaged, a pilot could flip back the cockpit cover and jump to safety.

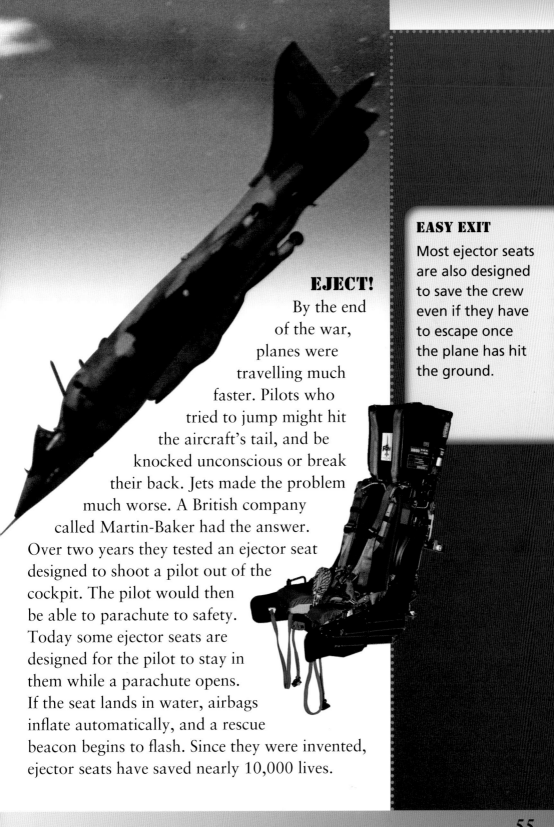

EJECT!

By the end of the war, planes were travelling much faster. Pilots who tried to jump might hit the aircraft's tail, and be knocked unconscious or break their back. Jets made the problem much worse. A British company called Martin-Baker had the answer. Over two years they tested an ejector seat designed to shoot a pilot out of the cockpit. The pilot would then be able to parachute to safety. Today some ejector seats are designed for the pilot to stay in them while a parachute opens. If the seat lands in water, airbags inflate automatically, and a rescue beacon begins to flash. Since they were invented, ejector seats have saved nearly 10,000 lives.

EASY EXIT

Most ejector seats are also designed to save the crew even if they have to escape once the plane has hit the ground.

INTO THE FUTURE

RAPTOR

This Lockheed Martin F-22A Raptor is the latest type of US fighter jet. It has a **stealth** design to make it almost invisible on **radar**. It is extremely fast and manoeuvrable. All its weapons are stored inside its **fuselage**. This reduces the chance of it being spotted by enemy radar.

Predicting the future is always difficult. What fuel will military aircraft use, for example, when oil runs out? Hydrogen gas is one possibility. For now it is too dangerous to use. In 10 or 50 years, time, scientists might have invented an engine that can safely use it.

IMPROVING TECHNOLOGY

As computers continue to improve, they will take over more and more flying and weapons-firing tasks from the pilot. Many plane designers are trying to improve existing fighters and bombers, rather than introducing new aircraft. But some revolutionary new designs are being tested right now.

fuselage   main body of an aircraft

LATEST DEVELOPMENTS

Modern jets have become more difficult to **manoeuvre** because they fly so much faster than before. In World War I a pilot could make a turn in less than half the time of a pilot in a jet plane. Both the American MMB Rockwell X-31 research plane and the Russian Sukhoi S-37 Berkut fighter overcome this by using an amazing new technique called '**thrust** vectoring'. Adjustable paddles of super-heat-resistant material are placed on the jet exhaust so that the thrust can be directed almost anywhere. This makes the jet very nimble. It is able, for example, to turn very tight loops, almost seeming to somersault.

PILOTLESS PLANES

The pilotless RQ-4A Global Hawk (below) may be the future of combat flying. The pilot controlling a plane like this would be sitting in a bunker, far from danger.

Is this the future? The Russian Sikhoi S-37 Berkut.

◄ ◄ ◄ ◄ ◄ ◄ ◄ ◄ ◄ ◄
Find out more about stealth bombers on pages 30 and 31.

stealth designed to not be seen

AIRCRAFT FACTS

Warplanes have been with us for almost a century. They have changed a lot between World War I, World War II and today. The aircraft in the tables below are all typical of their time. The Sopwith Camel flew in World War I, the P-51 Mustang flew in World War II and the Lockheed Martin F-16 is used in combat today.

In 1944 Flight-Sergeant Nicholas Alkemade fell 5485 m (18,000 ft) from a blazing RAF Lancaster bomber without a parachute.

PERFORMANCE

	Sopwith Camel	P-51	F-16
Top speed	180 km/h (112 mph)	703 km/h (437 mph)	Mach 2 at altitude
Maximum altitude	5790 m (19,000 ft)	12,770 m (41,900 ft)	15,239 m (50,000 ft)
Range	483 km (300 miles)	3350 km (2080 miles)	3800 km (2360 miles)

The Sopwith Camel was the best fighter plane of World War I but it was tricky to fly. More pilots were killed while still learning to fly it than were killed flying it in combat.

The youngest person ever to qualify as a military pilot was Thomas Dobney, aged 15 years and 5 months, in 1941. He was really only 14 when he joined the RAF but he lied about his age and got away with it.

altitude   height above sea level

TECHNOLOGY

	Sopwith Camel	P-51	F-16
Wings	Biplane	Monoplane	Swept-back wings
Engine	130 **horse power** **internal combustion** engine turns a **propeller**	1695 horse power internal combustion engine turns a propeller	Jet engine produces **thrust**
Crew	One, in open cockpit	One, in enclosed **perspex** cockpit	One or two, in enclosed perspex cockpit with ejector seat(s)
Shape	Chunky shape. Fixed **landing gear** (undercarriage) that could not be raised inside the plane	Smoother shape. Retractable landing gear raised into plane after take-off	Ultra-smooth design, including retractable landing gear to cut down wind resistance

WEAPONS

	Sopwith Camel	P-51	F-16
Guns	Two **machine guns** mounted behind the propeller	Six heavy machine guns mounted inside the wings	Single **cannon** in the nose
Bombs	None	Two large bombs or five small rockets	Up to nine air-to-air or air-to-surface missiles or bombs guided by **radar**, laser or infra-red **guidance** systems

◀◀◀◀◀◀◀◀◀◀◀◀◀◀◀◀◀◀◀◀◀◀◀

Find out more about these aircraft on pages 12, 14 and 17.

horse power technical term for a unit of measurement used to show the power of an engine

FIND OUT FOR YOURSELF

BOOKS

Jefferis, David, *Monster Machines: Jets* (Belitha Press, 2001)

Lake, Jon, *The Great Book of Bombers* (Salamander, 2002)

Winchester, Jim, *Bombers of the 20th Century* (Airlife Publishing, 2003)

WORLD WIDE WEB

If you want to find out more about military aircraft you can search the Internet using keywords like these:

aircraft + bombers
'Douglas Bader'
'ejector seats'
Spitfire

Make your own keywords using headings or words from this book. The search tips opposite will help you to find the most useful websites.

WEBSITES

Duxford
Website for the aviation museum at Duxford, UK, with online exhibitions, flying news and special aircraft events.
www.iwm.org.uk/ duxford

Smithsonian
This website for the Smithsonian Air and Space Museum at Washington DC, USA, also has online exhibitions and details of aircraft events.
www.nasm.si.edu/ museum

Fighter planes
See all the great fighter planes old and new.
www.fighter-planes.com

Air displays
Lots of great pictures of aircraft and air displays.
www.sky-flash.com

SEARCH TIPS

There are billions of pages on the Internet so it can be difficult to find exactly what you are looking for. If you just type in 'aircraft' on a search engine like Google, you will get a list of millions of web pages. These search skills will help you find useful websites more quickly.

- Use simple keywords, not whole sentences.
- Use two to six keywords in a search.
- Be precise – only use names of people, places or things.
- If you want to find words that go together, put quote marks around them, for example 'world speed record'.
- Use the advanced section of your search engine.
- Use the + sign between keywords to find pages with all these words.

WHERE TO SEARCH

SEARCH ENGINE

A search engine looks through millions of web pages and lists all sites that match the search words. The best matches are at the top of the list, on the first page. Try **bbc.co.uk/search**

SEARCH DIRECTORY

A search directory is like a library of websites. You can try searching by a keyword or subject and then browse through the different sites like you look through books on a library shelf. A good example is **yahooligans.com**

GLOSSARY

aircraft carrier warship that carries fighter planes to near their target, like a mobile airfield

allies/Allies countries that support one another in a war. The name 'Allies' was also used for Britain, France, the USA, and other countries fighting on the same side (against Germany) in World War I and II.

altitude height above sea level

artillery large, land-based guns

billion 1000 million

biplane plane with two sets of wings, one above the other

cannon weapon similar to a machine gun, but using larger bullets

civilian not military

Cold War years between 1946 and 1989 when Soviet Russia and the USA and its allies did not like or trust each other

commandos small fighting force specially trained to make quick attacks into enemy areas

continent any of the seven main unbroken masses of land on the Earth: Europe, Asia, Africa, North America, South America, Australia and Antarctica

crankshaft part of an engine that transfers the power generated in the piston to the propeller

cruise missile kind of guided missile that pilots itself to its target

D-Day 6 June 1944, the day that the Allied invasion of mainland Europe began along the north coast of France

depth charge bomb designed to explode underwater, and destroy a submarine

front line place on a battlefield where the two sides meet

fuselage main body of an aircraft

guidance way of making sure a weapon hits its target

high-performance jet that can fly faster and higher and with greater manoeuvrability than most other jets

horse power technical term for a unit of measurement used to show the power of an engine

ignite start to burn

incendiary bomb bomb that bursts into flames, rather than explodes

incendiary bullet bullet that bursts into flame when fired from a gun

interceptor type of jet fighter that can climb and fly very quickly to cut off (intercept) enemy aircraft

intercontinental ballistic missile (ICBM) missile which flies into space or very high in the atmosphere so that it can travel from one continent to another

internal combustion means that fuel burns inside the engine (like a car)

km/h kilometres per hour – number of kilometres travelled in one hour

landing gear wheels and lower part of an aircraft that support it when it takes off or lands

lift force that lifts a plane into the air

Mach 2 twice the speed of sound

machine gun gun that can fire bullets in very rapid succession

manoeuvrable able to turn or change direction easily

monoplane plane with one wing on each side

mph miles per hour – number of miles travelled in one hour

nozzle pipe that directs the thrust of a jet engine

obsolete old-fashioned, out-of-date

payload load carried by an aircraft (that is necessary for the purpose of its flight)

perspex transparent, tough, plastic-like resin, used instead of glass to make windows or cockpit covers in aircraft

piston piece of metal that fits tightly in a tube in which it is moved up and down by a small explosion to give movement to other parts of the engine

prison of war camp prison where enemy soldiers, sailors or members of the air force are kept

propeller spinning blade that pulls an aircraft through the air

radar way of finding out position of objects, like aircraft, by using radio signals

reconnaissance keeping watch on an enemy's movements and strength

rocket-propelled has an engine which works by burning fuel and oxygen together in a combustion chamber to produce thrust

silo storage site

speed of sound how fast sound travels

squadron fighting group or unit in an air force

stealth designed to not be seen

strategic bomber bomber that attacks an enemy's home territory, rather than being used on the battlefield

submarine ship that can stay underwater

swept-back wings wings shaped like a paper dart

swing-wing wings that pivot backwards or forwards from the main body of the aircraft depending on how it is being flown

test pilot pilot who flies experimental or untested aircraft

thrust force produced by a jet aircraft to propel it through the sky

torpedo long, thin, underwater bomb that uses a propeller to push it along

triplane plane with three sets of wings on each side

turret low dome containing machine guns projecting from an aircraft. It can usually swivel so the guns can be fired in any direction.

vertical straight upwards

vulnerable easy to attack or shoot down, not well protected

INDEX